W9-AEP-074

Bury Me in Thunder

Sundress Publications • Knoxville, TN

Copyright © 2020 by syan jay
ISBN: 978-1-939675-95-8
Library of Congress: 2019953145
Published by Sundress Publications
www.sundresspublications.com

Editor: Erin Elizabeth Smith
Editorial Assistants: Anna Black
Editorial Interns: Maria Esquinca, Erica Hoffmeister, Kimberly Ann Priest, Jacqueline Scott

Colophon: This book is set in Adobe Caslon Pro.

Cover Image: Ashley Siebels

Cover Design: Ashley Siebels and Kristen Ton

Book Design: Erin Elizabeth Smith

SASKATOON PUBLIC LIBRARY
36001405101847
Bury me in thunder

Bury Me in Thunder

syan jay

Acknowledgements

Thank you to the journals where poems from this collection first appeared:

1001: A Literary Journal: "Finding Youth Among Drakes and Cumulus Clouds"
Bayou Magazine: "Protecting the Home with Iconic Portraits of Martyrs"
FIVE:2:ONE Magazine: "Time, In Names and Found Things" and "Young and Gaunt Wolves"
Frontier Poetry: "These Are the Witness Marks"
ENCLAVE: "Harvesting Fields of Remembrance and Alkaloids"
Girls Get Busy Zine: "If There Was a Child to Name"
Indige-zine: "Filleting the Black Snake, Acts I and II"
Naugatuck River Review: "A How-To On Blooming Bellies"
Phoebe Journal: "A Lesson in Weight and Thankfulness"
Poetry Quarterly: "Soft Boiled"
Rising Phoenix Review: "Below My Mouth" "Bitter Bones," and "Bury Me in Thunder"
Sea Foam Magazine: "Postpartum Grocery Shopping"
Shade Poetry: "Almanac for the Ravaged Seeds," "A Letter to Your Dying Birthplace," and "Creation Myth Along the Black River"
The Account: "Letting You In"
The Shallow Ends: "Perennial Hunting Grounds"
Toe Good: "Root Soup"
Words Dance Publishing: "Feasting on Dysphoria and Sparrows"

"Root Soup" was republished in Hypertrophic Press.

Table of Contents

I. Cumulus

II. Mature

III. Dissipating

*For my first poetry teacher, my mother. I only know
how to create worlds because you taught me magic.*

Thunderstorms form by a cycle in three stages: cumulus, mature, and dissipating.

I.   Cumulus

"I've always had a theory that some of us are born with
nerve endings longer than our bodies."
— Joy Harjo, *In Mad Love and War*

A PERSON BORN WITHOUT LUNGS

My body is made of absences,
  of meaningless gender, of a colonizer's
    language, of unbearable things wrought
      from servitude and genocide. My body

is an ocean of graveyards.

My skin reminds me of shackled
  histories, I am built from ghosts,
    tongues ripped from our mouths
      so they could not hear us praying,

but I am still trying.

My sex is unbearable, both witness
  and participant to violent desire. My legs
    have learned to open to emptiness, where these parts
      of myself are made vulnerable,

but still I am not immune to rages.

I have desired to tempt the exploring fingers
  of death, that blush with my suffering.
    My wide body has contorted to enact

ballets of filament and feminized terror, with a wish

for safety, equal parts
        human and held. There must be some term
            for it, when my broken-open body
                will give way to forgiveness—

becoming a full mouth, capable of breath.

CREATION MYTH ALONG THE BLACK RIVER

My mother is crawling through a forest of cottonwood,
       catkins sticking from her kneecaps like unworked porcupine
hides. I can hear her moaning, the low-droning

that shakes the roots beneath her body. She is giving birth
       to me here, my sleek limbs aching to protrude past her thighs.
Still, she keeps crawling into taller grasses where autumn

air hangs on her forehead. Tsiłkali
       and deelicho watch from above, scouting the expanse
of my mother's journey, the trail of gore she has left

to bring me to safety. My mother finally stops
       on a riverbank of irises, her final push into petalled sheets.
Yes, this is the image I like to believe—instead of the one

where my father was too drunk to hold her,
too selfish to be in the room.

       I like to think of my birth this way,

       in a cradle

of tender purple that bloomed and bloomed.

Tsiłkali: woodpecker
Deelicho: hawk

YOUNG AND GAUNT WOLVES

Remember these of summer-set eves:
grain silos as thrones, a sky

inked and toiled—sky space as fresh
       earth, an obsidian lake.

          Fireballs sit steady
on Albertan farmland; this is a quip
        about Mormons
            and scorched fields of canola.

          Breath is hummed with cicada wings
      beating, fog rolling into lungs
with smokestack pillars,
      each new hand occupying the other
        or a joint.

          My new girl tastes like limes
       and cornflakes, cheeks
   shivering a thousand
   shades of pink with a tongue

just as greedy. Our eyes act
      as anchors to keep this blue-
        collar town alive,
until we have the means to raze it.

THE LAKE SPEAKS TO ITS BIRTH

I hold caution between my young hands   I learn to beware
        of the imaginary lakes   and the houses
that surround them   their cloudy mouths hosting
        teeth of privilege and kayaks
that hang   in garages like strung-up deer

                delicacies   instead I learn to build myself
        in the ovular blue in the backyard   where dead
                grass occupies shadows beneath
        quaking aspen   my hand shovel working
                furious and small   still unable to break past

waterlines and hard earth   and I will learn to water my lips
        with my drying tongue   hope reddening
my cheeks   with sun-freckles and spots   I know in the evening
        my mother will fill the holes littered with my anxieties

                placing a tarp to hold
back decay from soaked earth   before it settles into the lake
        and the homestead   and our bed   still haunted
                by its promise of life.

MOTHER WARHORSE

Stepmother used to rock me in her iron chair
        and tell me that
                utility is the immortal cousin to beauty.

Her eyes were like fetched buckets of still waters, beaten
        powder blue—shrouded behind pupils
measuring dark spots in the sunlight. She had a heavy hand
that bruised my skin without touching it.
        Once, she filled pails with walnut shells
to dump into the troughs of the thoroughbreds,
        enacting herself as both plague and refusal
                to loyalty. I yearned for her,
mistaking her open palms as sustenance, my vulnerabilities
slipping the leash like an escaped dog,
where my sisters ran screaming
—seeking sides elsewhere, hoping if they
could pass quickly enough, they would not see
        the tender belly of my sacrifice for them.

        I am reminded of when I watched a small child
        rescue herself from a strong riptide
        in the ocean, pulling at her limbs, a furious pony
        crashing through foamed peaks, head a bobbing thimble,
        until she crawled
victoriously onto the sand and looked
        toward her parents, their eyes elsewhere.

Even then I do not know how she escaped the water,
    I recognized a child seeking approval.
Stepmother watched the scene unfold
    from her *Women's Weekly*, burgundy nails
thumbing the page, assessing the damage
    through hair splayed, mid-hurricane.
    I wanted to ask why she did not call out
    to the girl's parents,
but knew that history was restless, unable to stop—even with a girl
            grasping the land after near death.

A LESSON IN WEIGHT AND THANKFULNESS

I am born, netted between roots of cacti
and seeds from the mesquite tree, my arms
are weatherworn, and I dream of lighter
limbs, able to dance. Yet, I only watch
as time withers me to tallow and meat.
A woman has come to work my bones
into needles and scrapers for flesh-filled
hides and as the weapon she will use
to free herself of her husband.

                              I learned how to gather desert salt
                    from my mother, trading our granite tongues for
                         gratitude. I collect what I need from hollows
              we made, mice rustling between their new makings.
                    Now my elbows creak from lifting the stars
                    as lampposts. Do they not see how I am making
                    a map for my family to find home? I cannot sleep
              knowing who travels in the darkness, I have been lost
                         before, and would not wish it on anyone.

I protect my belly with tortoise shells and collected
stones, weighed into the rim of the plateau, as if
the hot sun pressing on my skin will keep me
anchored from my own fear. My wrists are pressed
among stones, and in this moment, I had hoped
to be enveloped by the pooled blood.

I am happy not sleeping, watching burned matter
above pop and fizzle like corn. The woman swats
away flies from my jaw, skin thick and sweet
like old jam. In the morning, I will be thankful
and sore for the ache we made. I am learning to be
grateful to those who will build a home from me.

PROTECTING THE FAMILY HOME WITH ICONIC PORTRAITS OF MARTYRS

Merciful mother closed the cruel mouth
and rubbed persimmon on your brother, his hair
greased with syrup. Your stomach was bruised
in six different places, the lower on you
the bigger they were,
exclamation points,
purple supernovas of broken vein.
      She rubbed salve into your palm until it bled
with her thumbnail etched into your skin.
Her laugh was wind chimes in a terrible storm.
        Your bruises looked like kiss
marks from angels, is what your mother said
and flicked at them with her eyes
till they oozed with the same relief
felt when your father left. She may be cruel,
but saints wear halos of thorns.
      You burnt a picture of her till the edges
      looked like smoky O's around her hair
      and carried it in your pocket, praying
      to it for the horses to come in safely.
      Your mother stopped taking you to church
      but you found the Bible in her bed sheets.
Your brother tried to lie to you
and said it had the face of Jesus in the bleach marks
but you shook your head
and rubbed the picture of your mother

until ash stained your little nails,
black eclipses that would not come out when it was time for dinner.

BABY IS A BLOODHOUND

He pushes your nose to the ground,
shaming the unruly dog, and then grants
    you forgiveness. You move on.

        The leash occupies your neck
        with familiarity, and you forget
          that any other love existed.

Your bones adjust to order, to putting your mouth
to the river, your ears and folds
    trapping the scent. You are made to hunt.

        Tobacco, leather, evergreen:
        all ghosts you know from your God's
        work clothes and whiskey.

You learn quickly that there is no way
to appease the sins of your God,
    always dying at a faster pace than him.

        You learn to covet small comforts:
        the worn and warmed mattress,
        two green spiders on the barn door.

The purple lupine God's wife planted
still grows by the kitchen,
    demanding anyone to try and will it dead.

        It has lived longer than God's first cat,

swept up by a hawk, the sun bright
enough to turn laundry to snow-peak.

These hasty ends mesmerized you,
and you thought of them while working,
    busier than rifles in springtime.

You panted under the hand of your God,
devoted to his faultlessness, even as
you helped him collect his violent trophies.

FINDING YOUTH AMONG DRAKES AND CUMULUS CLOUDS

1.

I tried locating the epicenter of tenderness—its breath
caught between the bathroom sink & my ribcage. Peony
& daisy like lean-tos, hard stems rubbed raw against
each other. They reached up for my arms to cup their heads.

In the tub, you floated like a child waiting for baptism.
Your body rested on currents from jet streams, arms
radio signaling to places where I could not reach you.
There, I was just the earth beneath your play.

In the morning, there were mallards on the patio & you
admired the bottle-green plume of a single male who stared
back, beak filled with tubers. He ate greedily, body shivering
as it tried to accommodate more. You said you admired him.

2.

The fear you hid behind your back had begun to crawl over
your shoulders, opening the sliding door to the river, despite
your best attempts to wrestle them down. They offered
you a glimpse of your father, predictable with his anger,

making perfect weather for storms to flood the banks,
fast currents pulling us to the bus station, where you tried

to shake out the shells in your waterlogged shoes, insisting
we build a dam for your denial of the comfort you began

to learn from violence. You told me how you hit your head
on coral and saw visions of the fluid leaking from your body
becoming ropes that pulled you back to the cabin
from your childhood, and how it was removed of its horrors.

For a moment, you found relief, imagined a home
from exile. On the bus station steps, you tried to hold me
closer, but we were not strong enough to prevent the water
as it dragged you back into your anguish. I tried to build

us a boat from floating doors, keeping watch for when you
might float back, your hands full of pilgrimage gifts: a cigarette
you shared with my mother that morning, a strand of your
baby sister's hair, as if these convinced you of death's purpose.

3.

God pressed his fingers into the eye sockets of our city, bone-like
too cold, even when thick with salt & spit. He tore tree roots,
limp seaweed, & feasted upon struggling bodies unable to swim
away from your storm. When I asked him why he was helping

your destruction, he replied: I find myself wrought with hunger
too. When I finally found you, you stood on the only surviving
hillside, watching us float below—just as the farmer proudly
watches his cows come in from pasture below slaughter.

Except, our city was dying & you were its gleeful witness.
You smiled & lodged inside your mouth was the head
of the mallard, green feathers indistinguishable from algae.
Your body shivered, but God ate for the both of you.

HERE IS WHERE YOU ASKED FOR THE RIVER TO NAME YOU

and she named you fragility
and she named you aching
and she named you bruised kneecaps

as you tantrum'd against the currents, kicking
up salmon eggs until they made boats
of small and bright suns, which the birds

feasted on, delighting in their astral
violence. You asked for the river
to reverse your streams, tongue clapping backwards

like a skipping stone thrown from the lake
into a window—even the cornmeal
your mother used to make could not

heal your mouth, raw
from when you ate pineapple slices in the summertime
and their enzymes berated you.

I do not believe you
meant any harm to the cranes
and cattails; the shame was in how your youth
became a weapon. Even the river lacked suspicion
from your plundering fingers into her bed.

You bent so easily

into her belly as her teeth
investigated your prickled skin, as if the reeds
were mirrors you knew to dance in, to curve

      enough until snapping back into the faces of flies,
          perhaps killing one.

A HISTORY LESSON FROM MY MOTHER

1.

    Momma likes to talk about the day
    she came home from the adoption agency:
    November 22, 1963.
Just as JFK's brain matter stained a pink Chanel suit
(made of wool boucle, double-breasted, with strawberry
and navy trim),
        my mother was being driven
            to her first home. Her new mother

would later recall as it being

      the best and worst day of her life.

2.

Momma tells me how she grew up a few blocks
    from Doug Hopkins of The Gin Blossoms. She remembers the day
    he died, same year my second sister was born.

She holds sadness like a soft jar in her arms,
talks about how sweet he was:

    "It was just too much, you know?"

Sharing a look of complicity, looking out the window
and sighing before asking only herself:

"I wonder how his family is doing."

There is it—a thunderclap,
the upheaval of remembrance,
where memory exists, then corrupts itself.

HARVESTING FIELDS OF REMEMBRANCE AND ALKALOIDS

How your voice fades through fields
of poppy as you work,
thighs surrounded by floral blood.
It is all violent, splatter from earthly
exit wounds. Our mother told us

poppies are red snakes who have
learned to dance on land.

She says
that they speak into the soil while digging
roots to lay eggs. We dance in large circles,
creating a home for our footprints, wondering
if the snakes know we are praying with them too.

When you begin to bleed from between
your legs, you say you are feeding the soil
already turned crimson and burst-vein.

Our mother's best beading protects
our waists that hold the seeds we gather,
while we scuttle like silverfish among rows
of a corrupted sunset—we beg
our mother not to send us home
until the rain is everywhere and dancing.

But, as soon as we hear her whistle from the porch,

our heels turn up dirt as we rush
        toward her arms, offering our bounty.

MY BROTHER DOES NOT KNOW HE IS FRAGILE

He is playing on your knees, like the sweet boy he is.
Call his hands gentle, instead of bone-breakers.
Know he is a vessel of force, an angered sunrise pulsing
orange against unsettling gray. He could hold a twister
inside of him and never speak of it. He is a compromise
of a wounded mother, a rotting father. Born into the sights
of a hawk, waiting to be fed the injured and weak.
See how he holds the metal chain in his small grip?
What strength, what violence that lies untapped.
Call it gunfire and pleading for the fists to stop.
Call him recovery when he runs back in from the rain
outside, shoes wet, face red and heaving. He knows
how glee opens his lungs as he watches a bird hit the window
at breakfast. Call him a doting audience to the end.
He says he only knows dreams as a knife, as rabid teething.
Remember how he once killed the blue nights in October,
turned on all the lights in his room, declared the sun
as an everlasting scar in his palace. Call it bloodletting his fear,
turning it on its side and using the scalpel to pull its weeping parts.
Say he only knows about the resurrections, but not the dead.
As the first boy to know war, he says he is a hungry bullet,
but he only knows the first part to the Icarus myth.
He never let you tell him the end.

A LETTER TO YOUR DYING BIRTHPLACE

Embrace the damp fur of home, with lungs perforated
by decay and oak. Bury your face in his mane, feel
the old teeth brushing your hairline. This is your corrupted
hound: a braying half acre of tobacco leaf and wrought

iron ribcage. He is too large for your arms to curl around.
Ride him like the wild sheep until the bell sounds, releasing
yourself back into the soft dust and your mother's brave
and public embrace. Never forget the people who once

low-burned the grass to feed the earth, their homes west
past the railway tracks. This is the path your cousins took
on the way home from school, now serving as the linear
graveyard for the eldest with body embedded in a metal

mouth. This is the tributary between the high corn
and a supermarket. You could bury yourself into the lungs
of the old beast, the sad hero of mangy hides. The dirt
clotted in his fur unwashable from your nails.

Forget this all had a future—it was long buried
by fathers unable to save their coal and bourbon-kiss.
You will never look as good as when you wore overalls,
hair thick with grease like your hometown hound.

Despite sharing his animal body, you will never see how
the night falls behind his canines, the lockjaw of holding on

for dear life. Do try to remember: even the dying will fight until he is left with a clipped ear, right eye sewn-closed.

THE INFANT MACHINE

In 1853, John Murray Spear tried to create the New Motive Power, a mechanical Messiah intended to herald a new era of utopia.

A man once tried to give birth to Jesus
from copper batteries and his New Mary.
        His child did not wake,
    and he dismantled the bones, spine and ribcage.

    Did you know the man believed in "Pow-Wow"
        doctors? Amish, Dunkers, and Mennonites acting
as an imagined bridge between theology and medicine,
    tools crafted from theft.

        They will never know how a powwow
    drum can heal my heartache, the thunder
of singing and taut skin sweeping pain from the lungs.
        While my people were beaten for speaking
    our language, white men drained the blood

from our stolen mother, hoping to gain
    knowledge we have held since the beginning,
even the land could recognize our thankfulness
        while we ground corn and painted the sand.

The man and his failed infant, both undead
    in faith, did not have the uncle who taught me

how to find my lost wallet. The man who handed
me a book of matches, told me throw one in all
corners of the house until it returned.

My uncle, the healer who taught me to mourn,
though I cannot speak of his magic. Too many times
our stories and relationships have been stolen. To ask
of my faith, you will not have my permission,
my uncle still mourns a mother whose hair
was cut and had her name stolen.

The machine could never be alive, dreams of infancy forgotten,
its metal lungs undeserving of the air
after the sky has wet it, the scent of cedar lingering

on its copper eyelashes. Perhaps the young mouth froze mid-
inhale, knowing its thieved skeleton could not contain ceremony.

IF THERE WAS A CHILD TO NAME

There is a cavity in my tooth and it needs to be pulled
from all those men I've been gnashing away
at like the bubblegum I chewed in the shower,
black water surrounding my feet
from when I knelt in the tub,
       and my sister dyed my hair.

I felt like I was sinking in warm wet tar pits
and thought how La Brea would be a pretty name
for a child, put together, with strong fists
to sink men, suffocate them.
I would want this child dangerous.
       So no one
       could hurt them.
       Their mouth a deep and plunging
cavern, full of fingers to pull violence in, swallow it
whole like sweet things—the way water is cool
velvet cycling down a throat, an ocean spillway
filled with trash, or an empty sink that smells
            of mold and lemon soap.

II. Mature

"My knee is wounded so badly that I limp constantly, anger is my crutch, I hold myself
upright with it, my knee is wounded, see, how I am still walking."
— Chrystos, *I Walk in the History of My People*

A HOW-TO ON BLOOMING BELLIES

I cracked black eggs on the headboard,
baking them in bad dreams to feed
the dogs that run along
the fence when I walk to the bus stop.

My fingers are full of grease that the boys
                love to have run through their hair
            until they look like men who practice
                  rolling cigarettes
            and touch themselves when imagining
        their bodies being crushed beneath the heels of women
               with tight hair, dark brows,
who have crowns of war and the disparaged looks
of the mother looking through the car's rear
view mirror.
               They come through doors
        with streaked scalps, my skirt
        marked in lines that resemble tar bubbling
        on hot summer days—the tacky
black when rubbed between thumb and pointer
feels soft and warm, it is the moaning
of dinosaur bones being fracked until they blister pale blue.

        I collected the dreams found in loose hairs,
        on the quilt lying on the back of the sofa,
        twisting their ends until it became a braid—a rope
and I swung it upon the earth to fill it with wishbones.

My lover in bed
tried to make me daisy chains from the
papers
the boys had emptied, I held it
and saw my dying in their petals,
when I cried—the body of a whale
broke open, and my daughter emerged from its stomach.

WHAT THE HILLS LOOK LIKE AT NIGHT

Grandmother said that the spirits in the mountains
      were lovely, dark, and deep. But, I was bleeding

         all over the kitchen, so she handed
me a rag to not ruin the linoleum.
      I brined my wounded
           hand at the table, rubbing salt
into the flesh, before it turned

and spoiled. She spoke of monsters, and of great snakes,
      while I wondered
         how many pearls from oysters

           would need to be gathered in order
        to pay for my quick funeral.
The smoke from summer wildfires rolled in
black clouds behind my grandmother's

           head, her thick arms chasing
        the blue-bellied lizards under the pots
         kept on the porch. Each time she opened
the side door, one would race

in, eager with hope. That night, I returned
      to find the creature, rubbing its squirming stomach
         under my thumb. I thought of the suit

my grandfather might have been buried in,
Navy blue boy, who jumped from yucca to yucca until
he found a new home beyond a great canyon.

Grandmother found me in the kitchen,
and swept at the floor with her broom,
exorcising the temporary squatter,

and came to hold my hand. Everyone lives in the dark,
she said, everything bleeds. As we sat to watch
fire take the mountains, the blood

on my bandaged hand blossomed into three peaks.

BITTER BONES

Bundle your shirts in deerskin,
       take them to the edge of the ocean,
       throw them in the water,
    for your selfishness and grievances with death.

    Reject who deny your existence. They find you less threatening,
    born to be the mirror of your neglectful father.
       They do not know how you carried matches
       in your shoes, ready to strike up everyone.

There are women who held the guns against NDN heads, just as much
       as any white man. They just know how to look good
         while crying, so no one ever bothered them.

       Remember to bury your magic under the tree roots,
    do not dig them up for seven generations,
let them ferment with untouched hands.
    Your grandfather would have warned you,
       about this world if he had not died, long before you

           were born. Trust in him,
           death has made powerful
           ghosts for you to talk to.

BEFORE THE LAND BREAKS

Remember to hide your teeth,
    my grandfather says.

    The sunrise glare is cold and bright, as I walk down
        the driveway, built of frost and stone. The air is milked
            with membranes from low-hanging clouds when
        I breathe in, there is coppered earth on my tongue.
    The land thickens under my shoes, as my body de-forests

itself among the lava rock and moss. I try to search
for remnants of the moon, still hanging in its paper-thin shadow,
its white roan body a stretched, unblinking eye.

        I await the figure of plague that scrubs the sky
        clean of its freckles, with greenhouse gases
        and atomic bomb testing. It steps over the fence
            with hands outstretched, filled with oil, a dead fish.

        I know I must eventually open
        my mouth to receive it, and yet have sewn my lips
    closed with tin thread.

FEASTING ON DYSPHORIA AND SPARROWS

It is almost October in the woods,
      where I am held at an encampment,
           my room full of heavy mountain
      air that hangs syruped on my jaw.

A man is telling me I am a woman,
      instead of monstering
      flesh, paled like wisteria,
      stacked with smoke that mirrors
      the ash held in his glass bowl.

                    I dump the remains to give water
            to the sparrows, luring them
              to my windowsill, catching them
              in my hands and stuffing them
          in my cheeks, my words becoming
      plumed with promises of absolution.

      The birds are so particular as they flail,
      their erratic song penetrating my wisdom
      teeth, but still I do not become wiser.

      The man later removes
      the scraps, sneaking
a plunged hand deeper to remove innards—
my personal now made public.

I hang his desire like damp blankets
                     on laundry lines, waiting
         for my bones to turn acrid and unpleasable,
passing the time by pulling feathers free
from my bleeding gum line.

THESE ARE THE WITNESS MARKS

on the body of my lover—outlines
      and discolorations
      where ghost-limbs
      and phantom-talks
      might've inhabited,

      but now have been exiled
            into our bathtub where she
      floats, undisturbed. Goosebumps
occupy her thighs like raised
fists through
worn-sweaters—even when

            I dry her skin,
            she still tastes
         of marzipan and old salt.

            And of course, fear still shivers
                in my ribcage like fettered rabbits
           before the snare snaps closed,
                  of how the immensity of her
                zodiac mouth entraps

      my existence. Her loud body
ticks like grandfathered gears,
      or a bomb,
         in our shy bedroom.

The storm of her awaits
the window   to be
slammed open, swallowing
cumulonimbus bodies and spitting them

onto our sheets: new and old
lakes that could not come
from a mouth like mine.

SOFT BOILED

My sisters used to tap spoons on my belly,
their mouths
making the sounds
of eggshells cracking.
       I imagined my belly splitting open with yolk.
       I fed the women of my family from my belly—
       a tradition, a ritual, a rite.
The only spoons in my drawers were scalloped, riveted and not often used,
I felt hungry but the hunger lacked a name.

          It felt misplaced.
       I did not remember
what it was to consume.

When my mouth opened in the mirror, it was wide as empty bowls,
only water poured out from them into my sink.

I laid in a bed with a duvet the color of spring onions,
even its edges felt dusty like the rows of my uncle's orchards.
       It made me dream of thawed earth, where dirt trickled out
       from between my legs. I would wake and watch sunlight baking the
       porch, hearing the hiss of steaming fat on the wood.
My mouth watered for nothing.

STRAW HOUSE

The exact coordinates of my vulnerable bones
      can be found in the dunk tank of the carnival
         that has come to my town for the past 3,000

      years. Mama says that Marco Polo told stories
to Kublai Khan about our town
      with the carnival, while they both withered

      in royal garden, watching the empire fall.
         And here, standing to survive it all,
      is old popcorn and sweaty teens on the ferris wheel.

Mama says she worked at the carnival when she was 16,
      says she played cards with the bearded lady. The stroke
has stripped Mama of the woman's name, but she tells me
      about the bearded lady's smile. Such power,

         able to power each bulb in the big top, her joy too large
for the expanses of fabric to hold, billowing like clouds

         over the benches of folks
      who come to witness their own terror
and fascination. Mama tells me

      that my body is not a spectacle, even though I am part of the exhibits,
         touted on stage for men to fondle,
hissing with both fury and desire. The "Thing" displayed naked before

crowds of children, grandparents. I trust for them

       to see my honor, despite its denial. I send the new postcards
home to my brother and sisters, where I am tucked between
the ringleader and elephant bones, hoping they still recognize

     the horseshoe birthmark on my forehead, the thick brow, the body
begging to be its own. I know
     that my exhibition is titillating, horrific, that by my own volition,

      I could preserve ticket sales
         for the carnival for at least two decades,
but I will burn it down before end of the summer.

UPWARDS & INWARDS

The human need to be watched was once satisfied by monsters,

but now we must tend to our own urges,

grappling our naked bodies like mirrors to the night—hoping

anyone might still swallow our reflections.

WHEREIN

My mother tells me how she once sang
    with Stevie Nicks in a bar. When she was young,
      before the cancer damaged her vocal chords.
      Sometimes, I hear her sing in the garden,

      a hymn she has kept to herself.
    She sings to the gídí in the window,
when she thinks I am not there.
Even when the broken coughs interrupt her,

she continues as if a phantom
has not opened her throat. Her voice is low,
    and shares space with both an ocean
    and a desert, trembling with desire she is afraid to

    hear,

    but that I recognize.

Gídí: cat

LETTING YOU IN
for Aaron

That spring morning when I saw you, a glass moon still hung

at the epicenter of the sky, a beacon of cornsilk.

> If I had come to you that night, I would've wished
> for you to carry me to the river, laying our spent

bodies like fish carcasses on the skipping stones, and I would predict
  our future: long afternoons with warm coke, two people sleeping
  on a twin mattress without a frame, our spines

  curved like mountains meeting halfway.

Instead, you burned porcupine quills and tattooed the high priestess
  on my arm—kissing it clean with your mouth, an angler's
  lips raw with ink and prophetic distances.

  Your eyes were pits of dried leaves on a summer
pool, a small boy becoming a fish.

And I see you then, sitting silently in a car with rain on the window.

As I walk back to the parking garage, I think of how you will learn

to study my mouth when I talk, and how when we sleep your arms wind
  around my body like a snake strangling a field mouse,

and how I will gladly welcome that suffocation,

offering my skin as a second sheet.

CANONIZING THREATENED TONGUES

& now there are women without language

       my mother unable to articulate nasal
tones   & I speak   unraveling &
stumbling to know the fullness of chagháshé

       when she was a child her adoptive
[white] mother threatened that if she was bad
she would be sent back to the [rez]

       & my mother didn't know what that meant
but   homeland   became a threat
or government allotted territory did
it was all kind of fitting   in that way

       she would teach me lessons
in her great-grandmother's rocking chair & we fell
in love with the corresponding ways a wound
can hold meaning   can hold tenderness

       that pain is not monogamous
& holds many lovers & when I was a child
I held my usual sets of guilt   that my mother
did not really have a   [mother]
or [father]

            but I could not hold it long
as sage smoke imbedded itself   into my hair
twined in the sunlight & drumming on deer-
skin hides   from when she had enough
gas money   to take us to the nearest powwow

& how we danced on the outskirts   almost
in the trees   just us   flattening the earth
      with joyous feet   & made-language
      to store the ache of our   own stories.

Chaghạshé: children

FILLETING THE BLACK SNAKE, ACT ONE

Black snake has its nose upturned;
crude and offering riddles in tar. It sinks

ankles and tears bones, birds
with blackened wings descend. Nothing
here can breathe, the snake strangles cattails
and fox sedge until they lay like barren

tongues. I have not drank in seven days,
it is an unconsenting purge, my lungs
are pulpous—pinky peppercorns of meat
erupting like alveoli cysts, an urgent cough.

There is a blanket covering the mouths
of tributaries. It is knotted like restless
children, and the fish scream in night
terrors, their eyes fuzzed over with cottony
black. A muskrat eats clove-turned-oil-rig,

I cannot rescue its flailing fur, my hands
are buried in nests of slick eggs. In order
to prevent more snakes, I smash the heads
of its babies, they pop like hot tar on boots.

I must protect the ghosts of giant earth
worms, whose homes are excavated
from stone, their ripples carved white.

FILLETING THE BLACK SNAKE, ACT TWO

I must slice each scale with a knife blessed
by ancestors, to kill the black snake,

it must be wrapped in ceremony
and unsettling rosy sunsets contrasted
against contemporary war zones.
The lungs of the snake are the hardest
to remove, fluid pocketed in each part
that is dark—wet asphalt that reeks
of maggot gut and molted skin.

I am cautious to not erupt the organs,
they carry the most poison. The snake shrieks
without sound, a thumping dullness captured
like moth flailing in pillowcases, its fangs
are pierced into my calf that is dripping swollen
and caked painful, a body thrashing.

Tremors are felt in rural Oregonian homesteads,
the news report says a 5.5 on the Richter scale,
they haven't heard a jubilant drum circle before.
My small hands wrestle modern monster,
I summon strength like trickster aunties who wield
baskets as shield, cedar as arrows.

THE HEREDITY OF HOPE

Creator is a winding sheet
around the body of colonial violence,
missing girls and women

        hidden in creeks and lakes.
We pray that the stars
        can scoop them in their arms
        and give them refuge—

for aren't they our most precious?

When we send up offerings,
        the room is marked
        by my mother's most beautiful

        nacre and silver squash blossoms.
        What if we can remember each one
        of the missing in the notches of the story belts
        we hold close during the long

        winters?

        What if there will be a day when
        the legacy of whiteness will
uncuff itself from our bodies?

We try to see salvation in the oceans

where fish swim between oil and seaweed,
who keep leaping to air,
     desperate to survive. The pain claws
       at its insides until the stomach
       breaks open with pearls,
creating genomes for a future
capable of being whole and healed.

A HOME PRONE TO AMNESIA

I could say I have eaten my anxiety like desire—
fruits from which I unfastened myself,
because my teeth were quick or skilled enough
   to know the meat of grief

my mouth tore into. Except I didn't. I planted
myself a field of giant zinnias, their stems

sloped as bodies do when falling or shot. Called
   it a garden of heavy heads, called it overthinking.

Perhaps this is what my mother meant,
   when she said that we could bury our fears
      as seeds, and hope they bloom into things
   useful and good. But even my mother
knew how the hunger of grasshoppers

could undo spring. So, I called on my lover,
to take the plow to my hips, flesh aerated in their wonder
   and sweat. I collected their salt, collected

their sticky and ruined gloves. Ones that once hurried
flies away from my dirtied brow,

   since yoked off in exhaustion. Perhaps these could gather
the crops I reaped, no longer trusting of the spurred
   and petaled kick of the horses, who ate the land

and were poisoned by it. I waited for the river,
who swam and shifted with threat below, to sweep

away the hometowns and memories with them, and reach up,
pull my name right out of me.

III. Dissipating

"But as long as you remember what you have seen, then
nothing is gone. As long as you remember, it is part of this
story we have together."
— Leslie Marmon Silko, *Ceremony*

ROOT SOUP

Parts of you were dying everyday
skin picked beneath nails, eyelashes
      rubbed onto your palm, blood crawled out
of me
with long extended and beautiful arms,
and how when your teeth needed to be pulled
they turned into camas bulbs and at the table
I began to pull them out
      your mouth began to look like a smiling
      spider and when we made love, you
      breathing
      between my legs, it felt like willow
      branches
      being hardened and snapped on my skin.
   You made me bleed
and when you came up for air your mouth dripped
with many things, of winter soil and absences.
I made soup from your teeth and fed it to our family
who relished your cavities. Your fillings melted
into carrot flowers and soon they smelled of gardens,
of dirt being worn down under warm stones. You laughed
and there was no sound but I imagined it would have been
like leaves
on the ground when the wind blows or the fatal
      drop of cigarette ash on pavement. We took your
      dying things to feed our family who was hungry
      and cried

with empty bellies
    but even all your dying things
        could not fill them.

POSTPARTUM GROCERY SHOPPING

I tuck myself into the refrigerator,
next to mason jars of pickled children's breath.
There is the butter lettuce I bought today,
I crouch and dissect leaf from bulbous and velvety
stem. I shove loose heads
into my mouth—the farther in I go, the less alive
it all becomes.
                  There is a carcass on a leaf:
                  a bug. He ate like a king
                  in a prison, his jailer a plastic
                  tub. I eat him too.
The lettuce has circular absences as I move
toward its center, the functional holes
provide air for my mouth that grips
green like paint thinner, hoping to shrink
its body, consuming desiccated calcium.
                  Outside, the moon glares in to try
                  and touch me with all her maternal
                  wantings. I want to whisk her nocturnal
                  yolk into my gullet. I hope to devour
                  my son back into my ribs, his vast body
                  emptied from me like jellyfish bile
                  on the beach, the same place where his father
        proposed. I wish I could have said no, in that moment,
as if it could have protected these nameless eggs inside me.

WHEN I RUN ERRANDS WITH MY GRIEF

My grief is a chasm that I take into town
        to buy groceries for—the empty pantry

        standing as mausoleum to its hunger.
We pick out tomatoes, a single grape, and a carton
        of orange juice. I am still not ready to fill
           its mouth, despite its aching

           tongue that grasps toward

my extended fingers. I dangle a sprig of mint
in front of it, as if I could absolve myself of this needy

child of pain. When we are walking between aisles,
        I am unsure where to look, but I learn

        I have the power to turn any hall into
        a riverbed of sympathy and uncertainty—
        my grief floating on its currents with lifejacket
        encompassing its tenderized body.

Despite my sore ankles, I am not ready to return home.
        Instead, I give in to grief, stuff its cheek full of
        fennel and compromise,

           reach into my jacket pocket
           for a tissue to clean the spit forming
             on its young lips.

PEACH SLICES ON BREAD

The food we split between ourselves mimics cellular
        mitosis,
the womb of it blooming, until at last
the insides are scrambled. I don't remember
our fingers knowing such want, but then again,

I often forget our fixed nature. They say it is primal,
        but we have given it another name:
optimism. The leeching pipedream that clings
to skin, air sticky in the sweet stench
of rotted fruit and anxious-moving hands.

I won't tell you that this place we have made is safe,
violence hangs just a peach slice away—
the knife edging closer to our fingers. I know we want
to start over, to make these parts of ourselves disappear.

I won't tell you about the grain shortages, the water
being poisoned and drained, our paradises full of mold.
Why do I have to tell you anything? Your ears are too hungry
to listen, even if it is necessary for you to know
about the nagging famine at our door.

ALMANAC FOR THE RAVAGED SEEDS

here the world is wildly inescapable
            its fun-loving fingers dipped
    in sunshine   with flowers that blossom like your mother's
scones in the oven   everything here
    is pristine   even in its violence   everything
            has a place   even if it lacks a home
                we learn that place

    usually means a graveyard   more than a front porch
            we know it will be years   before we have a backyard
    that is ours and ours alone   except for the stray cat
            who chases the birds

we let him stay   he reminds us of impermanence
        and the obstinate nature of the killer
                we still are hiding from ourselves
                    so we plant poppies
                        to create a garden of bloody
    seed and petal   disguising our worst intentions
            in the sweet smell and crushed
                    bodies we murder in the fall
                        and feel no sense of guilt   since nothing
            could survive our mercy anyways.

PERENNIAL HUNTING GROUNDS

I am standing, unleashed, in a field of wild foxglove,
     and see all their mouths slit wide into weeping
     sunset, barks stacked as woodpiles. We try

to reformulate their mouths into teeth-holes,
but instead our mother chastises our efforts
saying,

     "You can't save what's already been skinned."

     She ties our wrists again with knots of cotton,
     and walks us home. We bray as wild dogs
without comfort or community.
And just like Creator is to the Saskatoon,
we watch the corpses seep into the soil,
     pulpy blood staining the soles of our shoes
     in blue-veined violence.

          We itch our wrists absentmindedly,
          unable to remember if we have seen
          this scene before. Our mother tugs

     the lead a little harder, and we bound forward,
continuing to decimate the bodies we encounter.
     We wait until home to see who has the most
          petals and incisors stuffed in their socks.

I AM AT WAR WITH GOD AND HE HAS A MISSING HAND

Today is the third day I have caught God
feeding snakes to my young cousins,

their open jaws consenting to slithering hunger.

Their arms and legs
        swell as the beasts curl in their small
                stomachs, faith spackling their insides.

I have learned
        I cannot sustain them on the petrified houses of memory
collected in the garden, once built for me, now
        laying open-faced and empty. I lopped off God's right

hand he plunged into a row of turnips,
his cries scaring off the chickens and sheep,

the selfless blurring a line between the thief.

He swore to seek payment from my body,
now there are children swarming my legs
        like young hounds for hunting,

and despite my best efforts, God
has learned love and cruelty are close relation,
and has taken my cousins into his pack.

RAWHIDE FOR THE ARCHER'S KNOT

My aunt is running like a doe with an arrow
in her ribcage, her sides are streaked in cytoplasm

and platelets. The bone-sawed edges of the day
pierce past trees as we run from divine punishments.

We watch the sky begin to fall, with feathers fashioned
to look like bullets, but we keep walking towards the field,

where our uncles skin our legs to give us camouflage
among the salmon carcasses in the nearby riverbed.

We tried to make a home in the jaw of a bear,
where the angles of light through his teeth gave us heat

for the stove, and stories told with shadowed hands
that resembled skunks and lizards. The hunter dreamed

of standing on the edge of our beds, his weapon cracking our teeth,
collecting molars as cornmeal for bread and to spread in his fields,

his crops only imaginary bodies of food. Yet, here we are,
standing in the open meadow, waiting for the red freckle

to daub our hides, our ears pining for the whistle of released
tension in bowstrings. My aunt shivering with delight to run.

HELLO TENDER PURPLE,
    for A.

do you see it? The little deaths that trail
        behind our bodies, bruised skin & hips
                stretched too far & welcoming. We try
        to build homes in a world thriving
on the disappearances, our thinning into omissions.

        Your chest is a hub of night, & often I crawl
behind your ribs to plant constellations,
                I wish we knew the names of the stars
                in our languages, but instead, we stumbled
        with ripped & stolen tongues.

I know that each syllable clapping past our teeth
        is a bridge, a larynx of memory, with tumors
                of trauma pocketing its wall, for each moment
        of pain we have endured. How many days do we spend
        at the stove, firing another knife to
cauterize & seal our throats?

        We are learning
our prayers make for steady thread, laughter
        jingling upon webs like dresses of ribbons, made to reattach
our mouths, unable to forget we were born

                from the burned & drowned
            & buried & displaced,

but we have remained, still dancing.

       Even in survival as tragedy, the chorus
    that follows us is breaking defiantly into the wake
of waves cast by old & horrifying boats, our hands hurry

        in the collection of salt from planks our mothers wept
        on, seasoning the earth for seeds to feed our families.

Maybe this parable for hope is useless,
    but at least in this version of events, we have forgotten
        hunger from the stories we eat from our shared palms.

ODE TO THE GOLD I AM HOLDING

on my back tooth, the cap more precious
than my lips and spindling tongue
                that searches between the skirts of any person

who might lift them. The soft metal
                grinds in my sleep. My dead grandfather's voice

lives there. He whispers songs from his home,
                                and each night I understand him less.
                Just like Californian mines,
        I am depleted of my grandfather with the strange sounding

throat. I chew on foiled gum wrappers to feel
thudding on my gums, imagining the blood

                grandfather might have washed off sheets
                        dying or dead men—their iron

echoing sharply beneath my velum. I have stolen
rings, hooping over knuckles like gravity, pliable beneath
                        a warmed thumb, or eager teeth
                that seek its value. The riverbed

becomes graveyard to them, as I toss payments for grandfather
                to receive, paying for the passages he makes to lullaby

                along knobbed chords. Some mornings

my mirror becomes monstrous, pried-open
mouth daring grandfather to climb out from me,

daring to remember the words that knew his larynx. Pliers sit
on the nightstand, waiting for when the rings are not enough.
I only have payment for one last song.

TIME, IN NAMES AND FOUND THINGS

We don't name our girls with things that can die:
        flowers are too oft subjugated to murder, decay.
                But what happens when I am not girl
and not boy? Do I inhabit the name
of ghosted things, undead things? Even seeds stomped
        in the ground are capable of returning—
                part-chimera of magic and honey, a body
        painted in holy white and lightning. Come autumn,
there will be another birthday for the not girl and not boy,
        with name that of a crow's ribcage. My lover and I talk
                about building a house, knowing we have
translated ceremonies into unfamiliar skeletons before.
        I am still waiting for the resurrection of my body, planted
                in new grout and tissue, howling like an animal
        who has ripped their leg from a bear's mouth and sang
with joy. I pray to the great creature who lingers on the edge
        of the river, unbleached from the words of white men.
                Yes, here the beast is found purposeful and good,
        it does not matter if it is the not girl and not boy—you do not look
past the jaw that will swallow you. And yes, here is a place
        that exists only with song and tradition to take in loving things,
                even if the name of it holds death.

BELOW MY MOUTH

       is a river running cold
into fields of squash and wheat,
my belly is gentle soil, upturned with hands
      rejoicing in the rain that blesses them—
clear kisses from ancestors. I am white-capped
like snow and northern winds, good medicine is stowed
        in my hips, for they carry the earth.

My eyes are east-facing windows,
     delighted in the morning sun that cleanses me
       with prayers sent upward.

      My legs are grown from the ashes
of a painted woman, whose sons once fought monsters
on the earth, born atop a mountain where lightning
     scraped itself as oil paints of white across the sky.
       With yucca leaves to insulate my feet, I would walk

thousands of miles to cross the bridges
    to our holy mountains, where upon the rocks
      of my peoples' birth,
    the ghost of my grandfather will feed me
acorn dumplings, tulapai.

BURY ME IN THUNDER

There are dances trapped in my tendons,
I run rivers around them, streams and dams
of blood seep into stretchmarks like Nebraskan cornfields.
      In my marrow, there are wild horses,
      they are running, they are on fire.
      I am sent to the mountains, where grandfather
      said Creator lived, to help us heal. I walk

      to the center of our pain, in shoes made
      from teeth, ones smashed by boot and gun barrel.
      None of them are mine, yet, I am responsible
      for them.

        My grandfather said that the people
      here don't know how to sing
the songs that close wounds.

Even with my feet splintered, carrying the weight of ended
voices, my hands are still soft, absent from the dangerously
deceitful. I have buried ceremony under my fingernails
like remnants of defense wounds.

      Even burdened by the myths of a wandering womb,
      one that holds my ancestors' memories, I have felt

      phantom weights hung on my hips, like a child's arms
      or a belt holding beads, or hoops of rope waiting

to be thrown on the nearest mountain. I wish that just like in stories
of heroic deeds, I could kill the beast by tricking it to walk
into my open jaw, before closing my mouth, smiling.

SOME KIND OF FUTURE

Witness my ancestors,
born from a mountainous womb
       spilling into the desert with dried
            mouths and heads meant for a crown.

      I have watched my mother furiously needle
thread into stories, aching to unbury her family,

now lost into the rivers, lost into the weight
       of exploitation. Here, see her sew the aunties new
tongues, able to sing joyously while fingers dance
         reeds into basketry:

      birthing symmetry like lightning across Ch'ilwozh
during monsoonal rains. My mother can't teach me
       our words, her father stripped of voice and face,
         leaving her alive but evaporated.

         I whisper to her, gift her syllabic memory,
      showing her how ceremony originates from the heart
and lungs. I call to her—shimaa, my mother,

and I see her eyes flicker inward towards shimmering
       sunlight and her father standing beyond Dził Łigayi.

She dreams of leaping across
       canyons into the bosom of warm bodies,

I can see it. I can see her eyelids twitch
    and my bones thrum with longing. I know we can't un-die,

    can't be un-kidnapped, can't be un-violenced,

but I can hold my mother, her left side weaker after the stroke,
    and she looks to me, eyes pale as water

    and I swear I hear her whisper gową: home.

SILVER O

I dreamed of mother again. In a field where the sky
    rumbled and cracked, her body hummed
        as bees crawled from between her legs,

           coated in honey, dragging their bodies like poor

        swimmers in golden rivers towards the ground,
    where graveyards puddled at her warm
and dusted toes. She gathered these amber

        fossils and cried without sound. Here the thunder

    was laughter. I opened my mouth to speak,
        instead, my tongue jettisoned prayer with fury
           like hail on tin roofs. She winced, a scared dog

           hiding from fireworks.

        Her hair grew into a braid trailing for miles behind her,
    woven so tightly, the piece came out inflexible and thick.
The waxy sun touched it, pulsating as frantic lightning.

    The silver hoops on her ears served to hold the braid,

casting her shadow like an arrow piercing earth.
    She began to dance, hair banging on her throat,
        hair mirroring the dance of a great snake.

I grabbed the braid and wrapped it around my arm,

tucking prayers behind new spools of coiled jet.
Each time my arm becoming heavier and darker.
I smelled sandalwood and corn pollen:

the scent of my birth, and I began to cry.

She hushed me, inserting her arms into my mouth,
burying parts of herself behind my tonsils,
rendering my guilt into silence.

The earth opened its arms and I fell into its embrace,

hair as ropes on a casket. Her lips spit songs gentle as rain
onto my brow, in words that I did not know but felt
as familiar and achy. She hunched over the side of the grave,

gazing outwards as my body fell away.

Below me, I could hear rushing, the gasps of expansion
like salmon lungs after meeting the sky, then carried
into boats. I knew I was returning to a different home.

She could not come with me.

NOTES

"Mother Warhorse" contains a line inspired by the writing of Arabelle Sicardi.

"The Infant Machine" references work from *Lore Podcast,* Episode 61: "Labor Pains Lore".

The epigraphs in this book are from "In Mad Love and War" (1990) by Joy Harjo, "Not Vanishing" (1988) by Chrystos, and "Ceremony" (1977) by Leslie Marmon Silko.

"Before the Land Breaks" contains a line inspired by the poem "The Olive Tree Speaks of Deforestation to my Body" by George Abraham.

"A Home Prone to Amnesia" has lines that draw inspiration from Natalie Diaz's poem "From the Desire Field"; in particular, the lines "Let me call my anxiety, *desire*, then. Let me call it, *a garden*" and "And if not yoked to exhaustion beneath the hip and plow of my lover, then I am another night wandering the desire field".

In "Postpartum Grocery Shopping", there are sections drawing inspiration from the book "Fish in Exile" (2016) by Vi Khi Nao, with the line, "I want to whisk the nocturnal yolk into my mouth."

THANK YOU

Many thanks to Erin Elizabeth Smith and the wonderful team at Sundress Publications for believing in this collection.

Thank you to Vi Khi Nao, who saw this manuscript in its earliest renditions. Your guidance and support has been insurmountable.

Thank you to torrin a. greathouse and Anthony Frame for helping edit this book, and for your continued support and championing of my work.

Thank you to all the editors and writers I've worked with throughout the years and to those who were just kind to me: Eloisa Amezcua, Anthony Frame, torrin a. greathouse, Wendy Xu, Luther Hughes, Tyler Mills, Madeline Anthes, Lynsey Morandin, Dan Brady, Jessica Johns, Joshua Roark, and Sarah Clark.

Thank you to all the Indigenous creators, educators, musicians, and storytellers that inspire me: Joy Harjo, Chrystos, Leslie Marmon Silko, Louise Erdrich, Heid Erdrich, Layli Long Soldier, LeAnne Howe, Joan Naviyuk Kane, dg nanouk okpik, Qwo-Li Driskill, Terese Marie Mailhot, N. Scott Momaday, Lindsay Nixon, Robin Wall Kimmerer, Tommy Orange, Elissa Washuta, Waubgeshig Rice, Lee Maracle, Tanya Tagaq, Leanne Betasamosake Simpson, Tommy Pico, Billy Ray-Belcourt, Joshua Whitehead, Arielle Twist, Gwen Benaway, Alicia Elliott, Sivan Alyra Rose, Crisosto Apache, Jake Skeets, Kim TallBear, Tanaya Winder, Winona LaDuke, David West, Brent Florendo, Wesley Leonard, Frank Waln, Buffy Sainte-Marie, Jeremy Dutcher, Black Belt Eagle Scout, and Redbone.

Thank you to Arielle Twist and Qwo-Li Driskill for blurbing this book. I am indebted with gratitude to you both.

Thank you to all my Indigiqueer kin for being the reason my heart blooms each morning.

Thank you to my siblings, for surviving with me when so much tried to kill us.

Thank you to the friends who have been buoys of tenderness that I relied on throughout this journey: Natalie, George, torrin, Emily, Leila Grace, Ahsante, Jenna, Anthony, Tatiana, and Jen.

Thank you to my grandparents and ancestors for being my most powerful ghosts.

Thank you to Aaron. Your love has held space for me for 14 years. I am humbled by all that you do.

ABOUT THE AUTHOR

syan jay is an agender writer of Dził Łigai Si'an N'dee descent. They are the winner of the 2018 Pacific Spirit Poetry Prize and were the Frontier Poetry's 2019 Frontier New Voices Fellow. Their work has been featured with many publications, including *The Shallow Ends*, *WILDNESS*, and *Prism International*. They currently live in Massachusett, Nipmuc, and Wampanoag land with their partner. You can find more of their work at www.moiraj.com.

OTHER SUNDRESS TITLES

Dead Man's Float
Ruth Foley
$16

Blood Stripes
Aaron Graham
$16

Arabilis
Leah Silvieus
$16

Match Cut
Letitia Trent
$16

Passing Through Humansville
Karen Craigo
$16

Phantom Tongue
Steven Sanchez
$15

Gender Flytrap
Zoë Estelle Hitzel
$16

Boom Box
Amorak Huey
$16

Afakasi | Half-Caste
Hali F. Sofala-Jones
$16

Marvels
MR Sheffield
$20

Divining Bones
Charlie Bondus
$16

The Minor Territories
Danielle Sellers
$15